IN ONE TIDEPOOL

Crabs, Snails and Salty Tails

By Anthony D. Fredericks

Illustrated by Jennifer DiRubbio

Dawn Publications

Dedication

For Alexandra Ohl—may her world be wild and splashy!—ADF

To my husband, Rob, and my son, Zachary, for all their love and support. Special thanks to Amanda for being my model and my friend.—JDR

Copyright © 2002 Anthony D. Fredericks
Illustrations copyright © 2002 Jennifer DiRubbio Lubinsky
A Sharing Nature With Children Book

Library of Congress Cataloging-in-Publication Data

Fredericks, Anthony D.
    In one tidepool : crabs, snails, and salty tails / by Anthony D. Fredericks ; illustrated by Jennifer DiRubbio.— 1st ed.
        p. cm. — (A sharing nature with children book) Summary: A child discovers a tide pool and observes all of the varied creatures that make their home there. Also includes "field notes" which provide more facts about tide pool animals.
        Includes bibliographical references (p.)
        ISBN 1-58469-038-0 (pbk.) — ISBN 1-58469-039-9 (hardback)
        1. Tide pool animals-Juvenile literature. [1. Tide pool animals.] I. DiRubbio, Jennifer, ill. II. Title. III. Series.
QL122.2 .F74 2002
591.7699—dc21
                                2002003866

Dawn Publications
P.O. Box 2010
Nevada City, CA 95959
530-478-0111
nature@dawnpub.com

Printed in Korea

10 9 8 7 6 5 4 3 2 1
First Edition
Design and computer production by Andrea Miles

Dear Two-Armed Explorer,

Welcome to my wet and splashy home! Now, I don't want to brag, but I'm actually the star of this neighborhood. In fact, you could say that I'm a rock star. Get it? I'm an important member of this crashy, splashy place.

A tidepool is an exciting place to live. It's always salty, always wet and often churning back and forth. And some of my friends are really incredible creatures. Wherever you look you'll discover a rainbow of critters—red, green, blue, orange, brown and white—in wildly different sizes and shapes. We're an unusual bunch, especially the snails with their funny hats.

But no matter what we look like, we have learned to live together. Why, some of my neighbors even make breakfast and dinner for me—or should I say they *are* breakfast and dinner? This tidepool with its salty water and slippery rocks is our **habitat**, where we find food and have our babies.

You live in a habitat, too. Like me, you may be the star of your home. But remember, we're different too—you *have* muscles and I *eat* mussels!

Your five-armed buddy,
SEA STAR

Here is a coastline with pounding waves,
  Sea-splashed rocks and hidden caves,
With seagulls gliding out of reach
  And clumps of kelp tossed on the beach.
This is where a tidepool lay,
  Crowded with critters on a summer's day.

This is the tidepool.

A curly-haired girl with wondering eyes
  Found crabs and fish and a five-armed surprise.
She carefully watched the things she found,
  Dozens of animals all around.
A questioning child, she truly cared
  For the tidepool home these creatures shared.

Barnacles with legs so small
   That waved at the girl who watched them all.
In one tidepool, fun to explore,
   A web of life on a rugged shore.

These are the **fish** that dart and hide
   And find their food in the surging tide,
Near **barnacles** with legs so small
   That waved at the girl who watched them all.
In one tidepool, fun to explore,
   A web of life on a rugged shore.

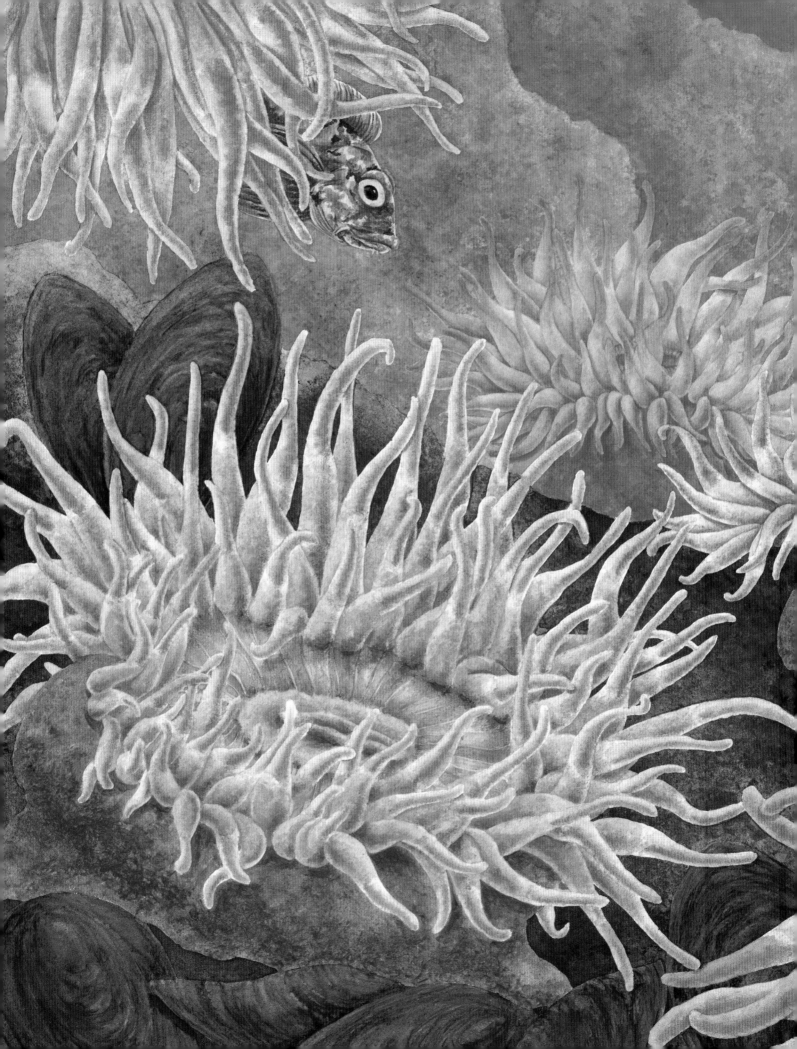

Anemones with stinging cells
   Hold fast to rocks and empty shells,
Friends to **fish** that dart and hide
   And find their food in the surging tide,
Near **barnacles** with legs so small
   That waved at the girl who watched them all.
In one tidepool, fun to explore,
   A web of life on a rugged shore.

A blood-red **sponge** clings to the ledge
  (a curious creature from edge to edge),
Close to **anemones** with stinging cells,
  The ones who grip the rocks and shells,
Neighbors to **fish** that dart and hide
  And find their food in the surging tide,
Near **barnacles** with legs so small
  That waved at the girl who watched them all.
In one tidepool, fun to explore,
  A web of life on a rugged shore.

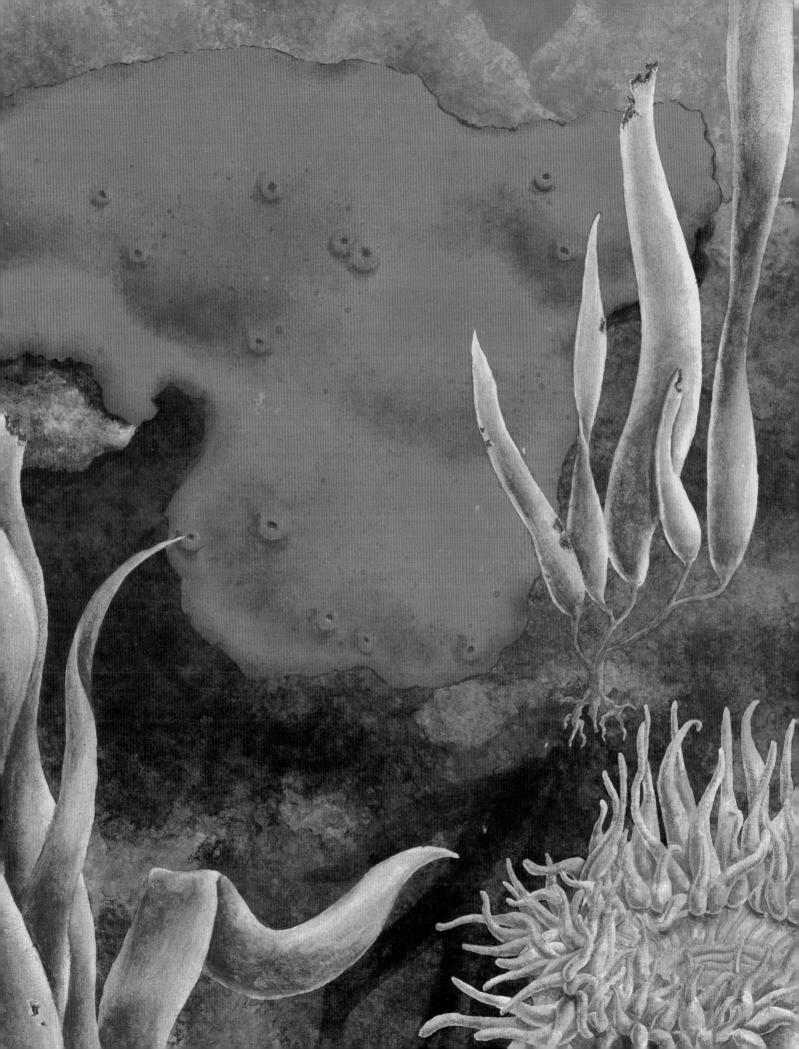

A group of **snails** with spiral hats
   Glide across the bumps and flats,
Beside the **sponge** upon the ledge
   (a curious creature from edge to edge),
Close to **anemones** with stinging cells,
   The ones who grip the rocks and shells,
Neighbors to **fish** that dart and hide
   And find their food in the surging tide,
Near **barnacles** with legs so small
   That waved at the girl who watched them all.
In one tidepool, fun to explore,
   A web of life on a rugged shore.

Thieving **crabs** drag borrowed rooms,
  Shuffling across the seaweed blooms,
Past the **snails** with spiral hats
  Who glide across the bumps and flats,
Beside the **sponge** upon the ledge
  (a curious creature from edge to edge),
Close to **anemones** with stinging cells,
  The ones who grip the rocks and shells,
Neighbors to **fish** that dart and hide
  And find their food in the surging tide,
Near **barnacles** with legs so small
  That waved at the girl who watched them all.
In one tidepool, fun to explore,
  A web of life on a rugged shore.

A cluster of **limpets,** brown and white,
   Cling to a ridge with all their might,
And watch the **crabs** with borrowed rooms
   Shuffle across seaweed blooms,
Past the **snails** with spiral hats,
   that glide across the bumps and flats,
Beside the **sponge** upon the ledge
   (a curious creature from edge to edge)
Close to **anemones** with stinging cells,
   The ones who grip the rocks and shells,
Neighbors to **fish** that dart and hide
   And find their food in the surging tide,
Near **barnacles** with legs so small
   That waved at the girl who watched them all.
In one tidepool, fun to explore,
   A web of life on a rugged shore

A knobby **sea star** slowly slips
  Across the pool on feeding trips.
It creeps by **limpets,** brown and white,
  Who tightly cling with all their might,
And watch the **crabs** with borrowed rooms
  Shuffle across seaweed blooms,
Past the **snails** with spiral hats
  That glide across the bumps and flats,
Beside the **sponge** upon the ledge
  (a curious creature from edge to edge),
Close to **anemones** with stinging cells,
  The ones who grip the rocks and shells,
Neighbors to **fish** that dart and hide
  And find their food in the surging tide,
Near **barnacles** with legs so small
  That waved at the girl who watched them all.
In one tidepool, fun to explore,
  A web of life on a rugged shore.

The tidepool hugs a rocky place—
   A magical realm with a craggy face.
It harbors all creatures, protecting each one
   In their own splashy world beneath the bright sun.

Field Notes

All of the animals in this book can all be found in tide pools along both the East and West Coasts of North America. The specific species illustrated in this book live on the West Coast. They can be found in the mid-tide zone—that part of the shoreline that is submerged for three-quarters of the day and exposed to air for approximately six hours each day.

Goose Barnacles

Barnacles attach themselves firmly to tidepool rocks. Each one has six tightly fitting plates. These plates protect the barnacle from the crashing surf as well as predators. They also help it lock in moisture. When under water, the plates open up and six feathery legs poke out into the water. Barnacles use these legs to strain out tiny plankton from the water, which is their primary source of food. The waving legs also absorb oxygen from the water. The barnacle illustrated in this book is the Acorn Barnacle that can be found on the West Coast. A common barnacle on the East Coast is the Goose Barnacle. There are about 1000 different species of barnacles around the world.

Fantastic Fact: The adhesive a barnacle uses to attach itself to a rock is one of the strongest known natural adhesives in the world.

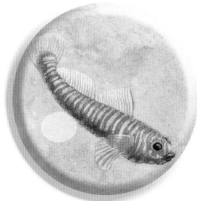

Gobies

Small fish are often found in tidepools. Some are young fish that will live in deeper water when they grow up. Others are small species that spend their entire lives in a tidepool. The fish illustrated in this book are sculpins. Sculpins are green to reddish-brown and grow to a length of three inches. They have small hair-like projections on their heads and four to six dark "saddles" across their backs. Sculpins live on fish eggs, shrimp and small crabs. Their flat heads and smooth bodies allow them to fit snugly against the rocks. Sculpins only live on the West Coast. On the East Coast, gobies and blennies are typical tidepool fish. Worldwide, there are 300 species of sculpins, 800 species of gobies and 480 species of blennies.

Fantastic Fact: After the female sculpin lays nearly 200 eggs, she leaves and never returns. The male wraps himself around the lump of eggs and guards them until they hatch.

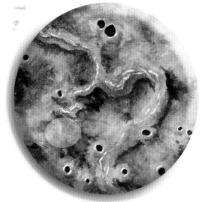

Bread Crumb Sponges

Sponges look like plants, so many people think sponges are plants. But, believe it or not, sponges are animals. Their color ranges from red to pink to yellow. These animals have lots of pores or small holes in their skin. The pores let in seawater. Sponges eat tiny sea animals and plants from the water that flows through or around them. Tidepool sponges form a soft sheet on the surface of rocks. They can be found in all the oceans of the world and are a frequent inhabitant of tidepools. On the East Coast the Bread Crumb Sponge is common; on the West Coast, the Red Sponge lives in many tidepools. There are about 9000 different species of sponges throughout the world.

Fantastic Fact: Sponges are some of the oldest animals on Earth. They lived during the time of the dinosaurs.

Hermit Crabs—Fully grown hermit crabs have bodies that are only about one to two centimeters long, but rather than make their own shells, they usually live in empty snail shells. Sometimes they fight among themselves for the best shells. As hermit crabs grow, they get rid of their old shells and go searching for new, larger shells. They can scramble across the tentacles of a sea anemone without being stung. They often hide under rocks or in seaweed. Their diet consists of plankton and tiny ocean creatures. They often have red antennae and blue bands on their legs. Hermit crabs can be found on both coasts. There are approximately 500 different species of hermit crabs worldwide.

Fantastic Fact: In some species of hermit crabs, a scale worm waits just inside the shell. It often shares the hermit crab's dinner.

Flamingo Tongue Snails

Sea snails often resemble their land cousins. They have a head with a pair of eyes on the end of tentacles. These can be withdrawn inside the shell in case of danger. Snails extract a chemical from the water (calcium carbonate) to build their shells. This growth is uneven and results in a spiral shell. Most tidepool snails scrape and eat algae from rocks or the shells of other animals. Some live on seaweed. Snails are often food for crabs, shorebirds and other snails. Some species of snails are also known as periwinkles and whelks. The snail illustrated in this book is the Black Turban Snail. The Flamingo Tongue Snail is a common tidepool inhabitant found along parts of the East Coast. More than 65,000 species of snails live in marine, freshwater and land environments.

Fantastic Fact: The Black Turban Snail may live to be 25 years old.

Sea Anemones (ah-NEM-oh-nees)—**S**ea anemones can always be found in tidepools. Most attach themselves to rocks or shells, although some species burrow into the sand. Anemones eat plankton, shrimp, certain fish and other small animals. When feeding they fold their tentacles inward, pulling the food in to a central mouth opening. Stinging cells on the tentacles protect anemones from predators. These cells, known as nematocysts, often feel sticky to humans, but are typically harmless. Some fish hide among the tentacles and are also protected from predators. Anemones move very slowly—almost snail-like—by gliding across rocks or by pulling themselves forward with their tentacles. Anemones come in a rainbow of colors including green, brown, blue, white, pink, purple, and red. Some individuals may live to be more than 100 years old. Anemones are found on both coasts. There are more than 1000 species of sea anemones throughout the world.

Fantastic Fact: Some of the green color in anemones is due to tiny one-celled plants. These miniature plants live in the tentacles and provide the animals with oxygen.

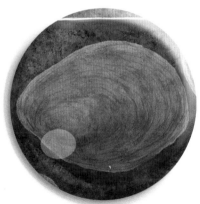

Owl Limpets

Limpets are mollusks with flat or conical one-piece shells. Mollusks are a group of soft-bodied animals that includes snails, octopuses and squids. Limpets can be found clinging to rocks. Some species live high in the intertidal zone. Other species cling to kelp strands deep in tidal pools. Most limpets eat algae. They scrape algae from the rocks with tongues that have hundreds of teeth. Limpets range in size from 2 cm to 10 cm. They usually spend their entire lifetime (10 to 15 years) in the same spot. They can be found in tidepools on both coasts. Worldwide, there are nearly 33,000 species of limpets.

Fantastic Fact: If the Owl Limpet is disturbed, it will defend its territory by slowly "bulldozing" intruders off its rock.

Sea Stars Sea stars are also known as starfish, although they are not fish. They frequently cling under rock ledges, on rocky shelves or on seaweed mats. Sea stars prefer to live where there are large collections of shellfish—which they often eat. These shellfish may include mussels, clams or oysters. Sea stars have a range of colors including red, orange, brown, yellow, green, blue or purple. Most sea stars have five legs, but a few varieties have as many as 50 legs. On the underside of each leg are rows of tiny tubes called tube feet. These feet are actually hollow cylinders filled with water. A sea star moves by expanding and contracting these tube feet. Most East Coast sea stars have five legs. The Sunflower Star, which lives in West Coast tidepools, has 24 legs. The sea star illustrated in this book is the Knobby Star. Found throughout the world, there are over 2,000 species of sea stars.

Fantastic Fact: A sea star eats by pulling apart the two shells of a clam or mussel. Then it inserts its stomach inside the victim and digests it inside its own shell.

How to Learn More

Dear Reader,

Ecology is the study of animals and their environment. Here are some of my favorite resources about seashore ecology:

Anthology for the Earth (1998) edited by Judy Allen, a wonderful collection of art, essays and poetry about planet Earth.

This is the Sea that Feeds Us (1998) by Robert Baldwin, a rhythmic and colorful book about special creatures in the ocean.

Along the Seashore (1997) by Ann Cooper, a delightful book that provides vivid descriptions of life in places where land meets the ocean.

Seashells by the Seashore (2002) by Marianne Berkes, a rhythmic book full of wonder and delight about some magical discoveries at the edge of the sea.

Seashore Babies (1997) by Kathy Darling, an amazing collection of animals that live near the edge of the sea.

Hidden Worlds: Looking Through a Scientist's Microscope (2001) by Stephen Kramer, an examination of the hidden worlds of nature including seashore life.

Sand (2000) by Ellen Prager, includes almost everything you ever wanted to know about sand including how its made, what's in it and different types.

Beach Day (2001) by Karen Roosa, brief rhymed stanzas describe one family's perfect day at the beach, complete with sandy knees and snapping sails.

The Seashore (2001) by Angela Wilkes, a book that introduces a dazzling array of critters and creatures in a dynamic place.

Here are some of the other children's books I've written.

Bloodsucking Creatures (2002), an examination of some of nature's most amazing animals—those that live on a diet of blood.

Elephants for Kids (1999), the story about elephants and their lives as told through the eyes of a 10-year-old boy.

Tsunami Man: Learning About Killer Waves with Walter Dudley (2002), a look at one of nature's most misunderstood natural disasters.

Under One Rock (2001), a rhythmic description of the colorful creatures that live together beneath a single rock.

Weird Walkers (2000), a book about a lizard that walks on water, a fish that walks on land, and an animal that walks upside down.

Your Amazing, Fantastic and Incredible Body (2002), an "inside look" at your own body.

Zebras (2001), delightful information and eye-popping photographs about these wonderful creatures.

Here are the names and addresses of organizations working hard to preserve animal habitats. You might want to contact them to find out what they are doing and how you can become involved.

Friends of Wildlife Conservation
New York Zoological Society
185 Street, Southern Blvd.
Bronx, NY 10460
www.wcs.org

National Audubon Society
700 Broadway
New York, NY 10003
www.audubon.org

National Wildlife Federation
11100 Wildlife Center Drive
Reston, VA 20190
www.nwf.org

Nature Conservancy
1815 North Lynn Street
Arlington, VA 22209
www.nature.org

If you or your teacher would like to learn more about me and the books I write, please log on to my web site, www.afredericks.com

Anthony D. Fredericks is a nature observer from way back. He explored tidepools near his native Newport Beach, California, the nearby Sierra Nevada mountains during the summers. Later he explored the high deserts of Arizona while attending school there. Now Tony appreciates the mountainside in Pennsylvania where he and his wife live. A former classroom teacher and reading specialist, he is Professor of Education at York College. As the author of more than 20 children's books he is a frequent visitor to schools around the country, where he shares the wonders of nature with a new generation of naturalists.

Jennifer DiRubbio is both a passionate artist and an avid environmentalist. She has been active as an artist for several organizations that promote nature and a healthy planet. Jennifer graduated with a BFA from Pratt Institute in 1992. She keeps her home and studio in Merrick, New York, as "green" and environmentally sound as possible, where her husband and young child also work and play.

ALSO BY ANTHONY FREDERICKS AND JENNIFER DIRUBBIO

Under One Rock: Bugs, Slugs and Other Ughs. A whole community of creatures lives under rocks. No child will be able to resist taking a peek after reading this.

A FEW OTHER NATURE AWARENESS BOOKS FROM DAWN PUBLICATIONS

This is the Sea that Feeds Us, by Robert F. Baldwin. In simple cumulative verse, this book explores the oceans' fabulous food web that reaches all the way from plankton to people.

Birds in Your Backyard by Barbara Herkert, can help kindle the spark of interest in birds at an early age, portraying common backyard species found all over the North America.

Do Animals Have Feelings, Too? by David Rice presents fascinating true stories of animal behavior, and asks the reader whether they think the animals' actions show feelings or instinct.

A Tree in the Ancient Forest, by Carol Reed-Jones. The plants and animals around and under a grand old fir are remarkably connected to each other.

Stickeen: John Muir and the Brave Little Dog, by Donnell Rubay, is a true wilderness adventure that transformed the relationship between Muir and a dog.

Motherlove, by Virginia Kroll. Animals of many kinds show the qualities of motherhood as they feed, guide, protect, instruct, comfort, and love their young.

Two books by Joseph Anthony, *The Dandelion Seed* and *In A Nutshell* are both stories—the travels of a wind-blown dandelion seed and the life cycle of an acorn—and metaphors for life.

Three books by J. Patrick Lewis, *Earth & You—A Closer View; Earth & Us—Continuous;* and *Earth & Me—Our Family Tree,* introduce the major habitats, the continuity of life and the connections between animals and their environment.

Dawn Publications is dedicated to inspiring in children a deeper understanding and appreciation for all life on Earth. To order, or for a copy of our catalog, please call 800-545-7475. Please also visit our web site at www.dawnpub.com.